Wedne

on old picture postcards

Eric Woolley

1. Wednesbury Park in 1914, showing the pond. The town's heraldic arms have been overprinted in the bottom right-hand corner.

£2.95

Designed and Published by
Reflections of a Bygone Age,
Keyworth, Nottingham
1991

Printed by
Adlard Print and Typesetting Services,
Ruddington, Notts.

ISBN 0 946245 45 2

Front cover: Valentine's postcard of the Market Place.

Back cover: (top) Pit bank wenches on a 1906 postcard by Ryder & Son. A bit of social history showing the girls complete with their billycans. A very serious lot they look, too: perhaps not surprising, considering the hard work they did. The picture was taken at the Blue Fly Pit belonging to Burr's Colliery off Hydes Road.

(bottom): Church Hill, Wednesbury

AT LEABROOK, WEDNESBURY   RYDER & SON

2. A combined canal and industrial scene at Leabrook in 1905 (iron works in the background) captured by the local printers and publishers Ryder & Son, whose premises were at Spring Head. Card posted from the town in November 1905.

INTRODUCTION

Wednesbury, once named as Wodensbeorg after the God Woden, is a place of considerable antiquity. It is also nicknamed 'Wedgebury' by many Black Country people. This book will no doubt be of interest to many people in and around the town and bring back moments of nostalgia to the population old enough to remember some of these scenes of the town as it was in "The Good Old Days".

Old postcards tell many a story and are sometimes a very valuable asset in unearthing facts of past life in towns and villages of Great Britain. In the *"History of Wednesbury"* by John F. Ede M.A., the introduction calls Wednesbury one of the smaller of the Midland industrial towns of the district known as The Black Country and also notes that the town was one of the earliest recorded places where coal was found; this item was a principal basis upon the development of which Birmingham's prosperity and development was founded. Wednesbury, though, was the birthplace of and centre of the tube industry, and the great strike of May 1913 started at the Old Crown Works of John Russell and company before spreading to the iron trades around the Black Country. As John Ede states: *"The history of Wednesbury is a part of the history of England".*

Wednesbury had three photographers who published postcards, and their combined work is represented in the book. Ryder & Son of Spring Head were the most prolific locally, but R. Price of Market Place and J.W. Bernard of Union Street also produced some superb cards — Bernard's strike cards are especially valuable historical material. Other cards illustrated are by Birmingham publishers, and a few are the work of Valentine of Dundee, one of Britain's top postcard firms, who covered the whole of Britain with their output.

Picture Postcards were first published in Britain in 1894, but it was not until a decade later that they began to take off, when in 1902 the Post Office allowed a message to be written on the address side. This meant that the whole of one side was available for the picture and obviously gave more scope to publishers. Photographic viewcards became very popular, and the postcard became the most important way of communicating news or messages, in much the same way as the telephone is used today. The years up to 1914 were the 'Golden Age' of picture postcards, when millions of imaginative designs covering every subject under the sun were published by a host of national and local firms. There's hardly a village or hamlet that wasn't documented at that time by a postcard publisher, though sometimes the number of cards available was unrelated to the size of a community.

Eric Woolley, July 1991

3. Wednesbury Market in 1911 with a large variety of stalls selling their wares. Another card by Ryder, with September 1911 postal usage.

Market Place, We[d]

4. A lively street scene showing the market with plenty of onlookers to enable the cameraman to capture the atmosphere of the time. The tram lines ran through the centre of the Market Place and shoppers had to be aware of any approaching traffic. Card published by Valentine of Dundee about 1904.

5. R. Price of Wednesbury produced this 1914 card of the Market Place, dominated by the clock tower built to commemorate the coronation of King George V in 1911. The clock is powered by electricity and controlled from the town hall.

6. This Valentine's card shows a view looking towards Wednesbury's Lower Market Place. A tram can be seen passing the clock, and next to Boots Chemists on the left, the Central Cafe can be identified. This card was sent to Hanley in April 1917.

7. A later card (1940) of the Market Place from Lower High Street with the clock again a dominant feature. Collins' shoe shop is on the left, and the road is strangely deserted: only a parked car and railway delivery cart are in evidence.

8. On 13th June 1923 Wednesbury received a visit from H.R.H. Prince of Wales. On this photographic card, the Mayor, Councillor Alfred Beebee, is seen greeting His Royal Highness as the distinguished guests look on. Card by J.W. Bernard of Union Street.

9. Another postcard by Bernard, showing the thousands of people who thronged the Market Place to see the Prince (the future Edward VII) arrive by motor car and approach the specially-built platform near the clock. Here the invited guests and dignitaries were waiting.

10. Ryder & Son published this card of Wood Green with St. Paul's Church spire a prominent feature. The only visible traffic is a tramcar in the distance. Card posted at Wednesbury in March 1907.

11. Holden Road was formerly known as 'Hangman's Lane', because the manorial execution elm stood there. No indication of who published this photographic card, posted in May 1913.

12. The library stands on the corner of Hollies Drive, with the main entrance just to the left. The shop on the right is not identified, but the name of Underwood of Wednesbury is printed on the sun blind. Valentine's 'XL' series postcard, posted in July 1917 to Colwyn Bay.

13. Another, later (1939) postcard of the public library, showing the entrance in Hollies Drive.

14. Wood Green Road on one of the many variations of postcards published of this main highway from Wednesbury to the Pleck and Walsall. No clue to the card's publisher, but vintage is around 1920.

King's Hill, Wednesbury.   Ryder & Son.

15. King's Hill on a 1904 card by Ryder & Son. This is situated on the parish boundaries of Darlaston and Wednesbury. The postcard was used as an advert for a confectionery firm and overprinted on the back, as seen below.

Post   CARD.

ADDRESS TO BE WRITTEN ON THIS SI...

Write here—for Inland Postage Only.

High=class
Cakes and Confectionery.

Birthday and Bride
Cakes.

Teas and Refreshments.

SCHOOLS, PARTIES, &c., CATERED FOR.

Jones,
Walsall Street Hygienic Steam Bakery,
WEDNESBURY.

OAKESWELL END, WEDNESBURY.

16. Although captioned 'Oakeswell End', this card shows a scene of King's Hill, with St. Andrews Mission Church on the right. It's a classic example of a rare mistake by the publisher R. Price of Market Place. Card used from the town in July 1911.

Kings Hill.

17. A later view of King's Hill (about 1950) by the Landscape View Publishers, Market Harborough. Rows of terraced houses and small shops contrast sharply with the more modern form of street lighting in evidence.

The Park, Kings Hill.

18. A section of the park at King's Hill on a card by the same publishers as illus. 17. The ground was once covered by colliery waste and was opened as a recreation park in 1900.

Post Office

PRICES SERIES.

MUNICIPAL BDGS. WEDNESBURY

19. Another Price's card, posted in December 1919, and showing the Town Hall and Post Office. Situated on the Holyhead Road, the Town Hall was built in 1871-2 but much enlarged in 1913.

New Conservative Club, Wednesbury.

20. The New Conservative Club was first established in 1886 in strict connection with the Conservative and Unionist Party, but the premises were entirely rebuilt in 1904, at a cost of more than £3,000, and re-opened by Lord Windsor. On this card by Ryder & Son, posted at Wednesbury in April 1905, the horse-drawn hansom cab appears to have been superimposed on the picture.

Conservative and Unionist Club, Wednesbury.

21. A fine view of the Conservative and Unionist Club in Walsall Street at the top of Spring Head on a c.1920 'Park' series card.

The great Wednesbury strike started on 9th May 1913 when 200 workers from the old Patent Tube works of John Russell & Co. stopped work without notice and demanded better wages. It spread to other industries, and led to many lockouts and much hardship during a difficult period — yet one that was an outstanding feature of Black Country history. The following five postcards by J.W. Bernard all highlight the strike.

22. Strikers' wives/children queueing for bread and other handouts.

23. The looks on the men's faces say it all as they crowd around a stall which again is giving away food due to the generosity of a fishmonger from Fleetwood.

24. Strikers pose for a photograph displaying posters *"we can*
tonight at the Palace, Wednesbury."

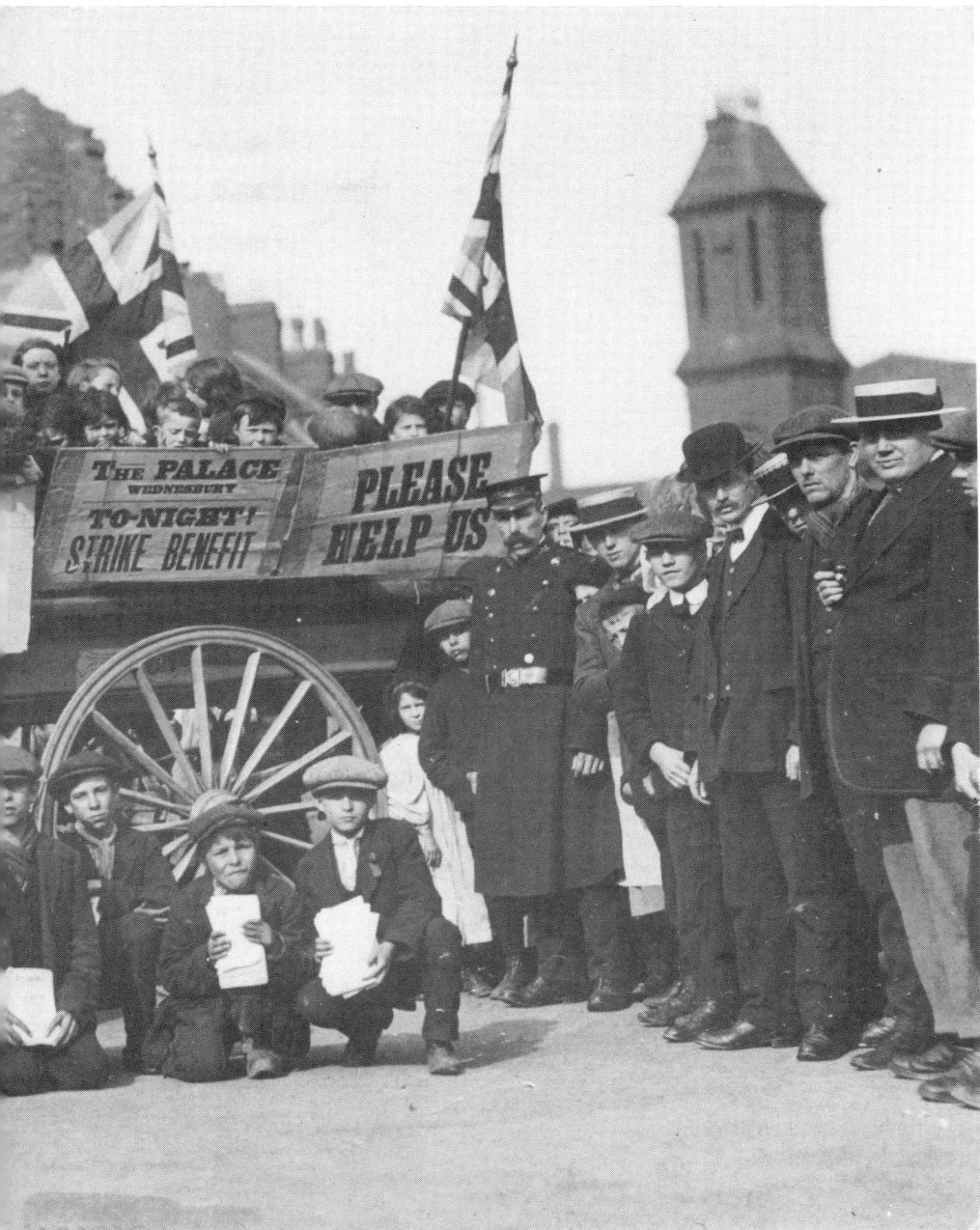

THE PALACE
WEDNESBURY
TO-NIGHT!
STRIKE BENEFIT

PLEASE
HELP US

it — please help us." Another advertised a *"strike benefit*

25. The children are not going hungry here, at a specially-arranged treat. The words on the placard read *"Keep on smiling girls; help one another boys; better days are coming; wait a little longer."*

26. A large group of strikers' children gathered together and photographed by postcard publisher J.W. Bernard.

The strike was eventually settled and a minimum wage for unskilled labourers of 22 shillings a week, and union recognition, were some of the advantages won by the striking men and women.

The five strike postcards illustrated were sent in envelopes in two batches, on 11th July and 15th August 1913, by Olive from 48 Pound Road, Wednesbury. The message spread over three and two of the cards respectively.

The first read *"Dear Jim, Many thanks for the photos of you while you were at camp ... the strike is almost settled now, I think they have had enough of it; they have been out nine weeks now. The vicar at the old church, Wednesbury, said to some of the men's wives that eighteen shillings a week was enough for any labourer, but the people waited for him after that, they went to church one Sunday morning and said to him they would fetch him out and tell him to feed the body never mind the soul, they had police to bring and fetch him to church the rest of the day."*

Five weeks later, Olive wrote: *"Thanks for the postcards, I should think your new house will look alright when it is finished. I wish we could have one put up. The strike is all settled here but I am sending you two more cards. All the men in the works had to work all the holiday."*

27. The Great Western Hotel in the 1920s. It stood on the corner of Potters Lane and Gt. Western Street. The famous 'Deer's Leap', the trade mark of Mitchells and Butlers, can clearly be seen on the sign over the entrance.

28. The co-operative society organised a children's gala in 1914, and local photographer J.W. Bernard took this picture of the crowds swarming around the Market Place. Bernard always embossed his company name in the bottom right-hand corner of the cards, but rarely used a caption with his work.

TRAM TERMINUS & HOTEL, WEDNESBURY.   G.5720.

29. Wednesbury's tram terminus was known as the 'White Horse' terminus because of its proximity to the well-known hotel of that name. Lloyds bank can also be seen on the extreme left of this late 1930s card published by Valentine.

CANAL FROM CRANKHALL BRIDGE, WEDNESBURY.   RYDER & SON.

30. This view of the canal from Crankhall Bridge is not one of Ryder's best postcard publications but is interesting nevertheless. It seems the canal boat might even have been superimposed on the card! Posted from Darlaston in August 1906.

Wednesbury Art Gallery: The Richards Room.   *Ryder & Son*

31. An interior view of the Art Gallery showing the Richards Room. Every inch of wall space seems to be covered with valuable paintings which were left to the town by Mrs. Richards. Her bequest prompted the authorities to open an art gallery in November 1891. Mrs. Richards also left £2,000 to help build the gallery, £1,000 for the caretaker's salary, and £500 for the regilding of the pictures. Postcard by Ryder & Son, sent from Wednesbury in October 1905.

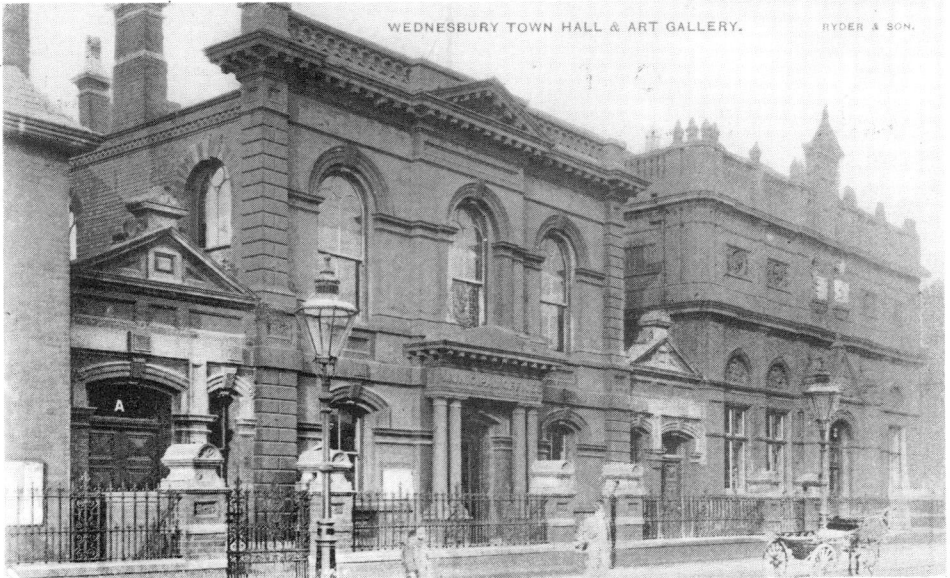

WEDNESBURY TOWN HALL & ART GALLERY.   RYDER & SON.

32. Another Ryder card, published about 1908, showing the Art Gallery attached to the Town Hall. The Gallery is still in use, and some rooms are used for social functions. Without doubt the most imposing building in the town.

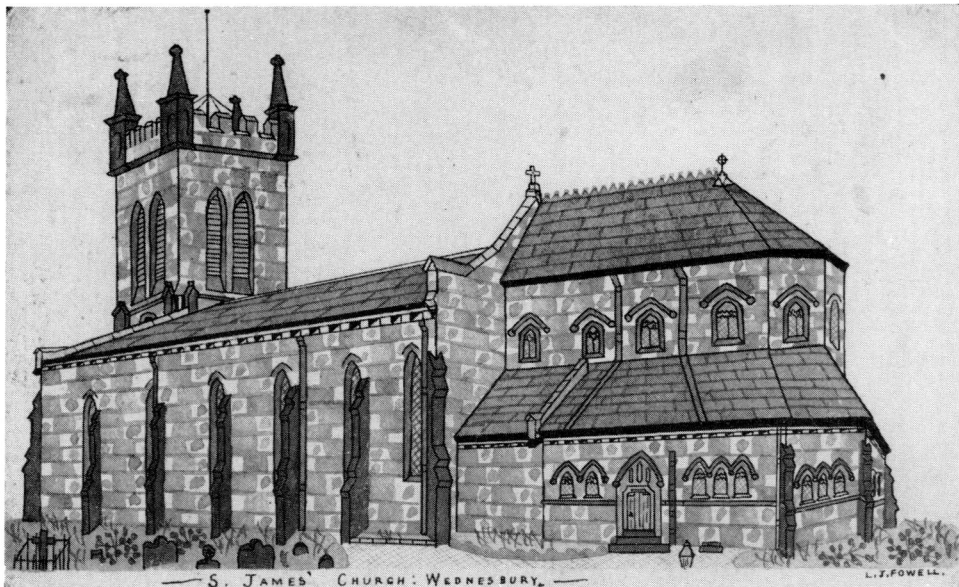

—S. JAMES' CHURCH: WEDNESBURY.—

L.J.FOWELL.

33. The church of St. James, depicted here on a hand-drawn pen and ink sketch by boy scout L.J. Powell, was consecrated on 31st May 1848. It cost over £3,405 to build. The card was postally used in April 1905.

"THE MOBBING OF JOHN WESLEY AT WEDNESBURY."

34. Postcard reproduction of the mobbing of John Wesley, the methodist preacher, at Wednesbury on 20th October 1743. The scene is probably at High Bullen, where he preached at least 45 times.

The cross indicates a cottage off Bridge Street, once the home of "Honest Munchin," a converted ruffian who rescued John Wesley from his would-be murderers in the historic Wednesbury riots in 1743. He died at Birmingham in 1789, at the age of 85, and his tombstone may be seen in St. Paul's Churchyard there.

Honest Munchin's Cottage, Wednesbury.

Ryder & Son.

35. The attack on John Wesley shown on the previous card was the fiercest of some 40 that he had to endure. The mob at Wednesbury clubbed the preacher, grabbed him by the hair and punched him. He was saved by 'a converted ruffian' called 'Honest Munchin', who dragged him free. Munchin's cottage, off Bridge Street in Wednesbury, is shown on this Ryder postcard. The rescuer died in Birmingham in 1789 at the age of 85, and is buried in St. Paul's Churchyard in the city. This postcard was mailed from Wolverhampton in May 1907.

36. Once described as a pretty, surburban church, St. Paul's at Wood Green was built in 1874 of red sandstone and partly endowed by the Elwell family. 1888 saw the spire, clock and bells added, and in 1904 a wrought-iron screen costing £100 was erected at the entrance to the chancel in memory of the late vicar, Rev. G. Tuthill. Postcard no.4 by R. Price of Wednesbury, postally used in January 1905.

37. The Catholic Church of St. Mary is a fine Gothic building, erected in 1872, and designed by Gilbert Blount of London. In 1904 a beautiful carved stone and marble altar was put up as a memorial to Father Montgomery, who brought the Catholic religion to Wednesbury almost single-handed, and to Canon Bathurst. Price's series card, published about 1911.

38. Another photographic card by R. Price of similar vintage, and showing the unusual sight of two churches side by side at Wednesbury's Church Hill. The Roman Catholic church is on the left, while the parish church of St. Bartholomew, originally built between 1080 and 1216, stands on the right.

Entrance to Wednesbury Park, Wednesbury.

39. R. Price numbered some of his cards — this is no.1, showing Wednesbury Park entrance, and giving a clear view of the lodge and fine gardens. The town coat of arms is featured inset.

2580. THE PARK, WEDNESBURY.

40. Brunswick Park was opened to celebrate Queen Victoria's Jubilee and was dedicated for public use on 21st June 1887. It cost £6,000, with half this sum going to the Patent Shaft and Axletree Company for the land. Card published by Harold Bott of Birmingham, posted at Wednesbury in August 1913.

A BIT OF BRUNSWICK PARK, WEDNESBURY.

41. This is one of the earliest view postcards of Wednesbury, published in 1901. A space was left on the front of the card for the sender to write a message, as only the address was allowed on the back due to Post Office regulations, until these were changed in 1902. On the picture, a group of children are obviously enjoying themselves on a day out in the park. The bandstand is in the background.

42. The main entrance to Brunswick Park in Wood Green is shadowed by the half-timbered building called Park Lodge. The card illustrated was sent from an address in Pound Road, Wednesbury, in December 1913.

BANDSTAND, BRUNSWICK PARK, WEDNESBURY.   No 8

43. A close-up view of the park's bandstand on a 1940s card, posted to Leamington Spa in January 1949. The conical-shape structure is typical of the Victorian bandstands, where the public were entertained on Sundays by various brass bands, including the local band from the Crown Tube works.

RIVER TAME at Bustleholme, Wednesbury.   *Ryder & Son.*

44. The River Tame runs near Wednesbury at Bustleholme, and the old Bustleholme mill can be seen in the background. This was owned by the Comberfords until 1594, when it was sold to the Stanleys. Postcard by Ryder & Son, posted to Derby in October 1904.

45. St. Mary's convent was opened in 1930 to accommodate the sisterhood called the Faithful Companions of Jesus. They were brought to the town by Dr. Francis O'Hanlan, and the convent was established two years after his death.

46. Another 1930s card, published, like the previous one, by Price, of the very large gardens belonging to the convent on Church Hill. It later became a convent school but was closed in 1959 as a result of educational re-organisation.

47. Women war workers at Wednesbury, 1917. Women played their part in the Great War while the men were fighting abroad. A superb photographic study by John Price & Sons of Bilston. *"What do you think of these girls? I have my uniform now, so I wonder would you know me,"* wrote Jack in September 1918.

esbury   834. J.P.&S.B.

Elwell's Pool and Forge, Wednesbury. *Ryder & Son.*

48. An early Ryder postcard showing Elwell's Pool and Forge. Elwells were a very famous family in the Wednesbury area, manufacturing hand tools, and their catalogue of 1899 listed over 1,200 different types. The business became a limited company in 1902, and amalgamations with other firms took place, for example with Wolverhampton-based Chillington Tools. Edge Tools Industries was formed from these ventures.

THE WAR MEMORIAL, WEDNESBURY. 10548

49. Wednesbury's War Memorial, dedicated to the men of the town who gave their lives in two world wars, is situated in the garden of remembrance in Walsall Street. Postcard published in the 'R.A.' series by a London firm, and used in 1955.